Missing

People

A Stunning Collection Of Missing Persons Cases And Stories Of Missing People And Their Unusual Disappearances

Malcolm Cliver

© **Copyright 2015 by Malcolm Cliver - All rights reserved.**

This document is geared towards providing exact and reliable information in regards to the topic and issue covered. The publication is sold with the idea that the publisher is not required to render accounting, officially permitted, or otherwise, qualified services. If advice is necessary, legal or professional, a practiced individual in the profession should be ordered.

- From a Declaration of Principles which was accepted and approved equally by a Committee of the American Bar Association and a Committee of Publishers and Associations.

In no way is it legal to reproduce, duplicate, or transmit any part of this document in either electronic means or in printed format. Recording of this publication is strictly prohibited and any storage of this document is not allowed unless with written permission from the publisher. All rights reserved.

The information provided herein is stated to be truthful and consistent, in that any liability, in terms of inattention or otherwise, by any usage or abuse of any policies, processes, or directions contained within is the solitary and utter responsibility of the recipient reader. Under no circumstances will any legal responsibility or blame be held against the publisher for any reparation, damages, or monetary loss due to the information herein, either directly or indirectly.

Respective authors own all copyrights not held by the publisher.

The information herein is offered for informational purposes solely, and is universal as so. The presentation of the information is without contract or any type of guarantee assurance.

The trademarks that are used are without any consent, and the publication of the trademark is without permission or backing by the trademark owner. All trademarks and brands within this book are for clarifying purposes only and are the owned by the owners themselves, not affiliated with this document.

Cover image courtesy of R. nial bradshaw – Flickr - https://www.flickr.com/photos/zionfiction/9963152475/

Table of Contents

Introduction	vi
Chapter 1 : The Leader Went Down	1
Chapter 2: Lost in the Indiana Dunes Since 1966	6
Chapter 3: Friends, Booze, and Phone Calls	12
Chapter 4 : Grabbed from the Cradle	19
Chapter 5: Like Mother, Like Daughter	27
Chapter 6 : Where is Zebb?	31
Chapter 7: Missing Photos	34
Chapter 9: Lost Lyricist	48
Chapter 10 : The Missing Film	56
Chapter 11: Gone in April	61
Chapter 12 : Lost Keepers in Flannan Isles	66
Conclusion	72
Check Out My Other Books	73
Want more books?	74

Want more books?

Would you love books delivered straight to your inbox every week?

Free?

How about non-fiction books on all kinds of subjects?

We send out e-books to our loyal subscribers every week to download and enjoy!

All you have to do is join! It's so easy!

Just visit the link at the end of this book to sign up and then wait for your books to arrive!

Introduction

People disappear everyday: some of them turn up murdered, some willingly escaped their current lives, while some cases remain to be clouded with mystery. Day by day, we hear and read about missing people, but we take them for granted because none of them are connected to us.

For the families of the people who disappeared, they are constantly hoping that the public would care enough if they happen to see a person who resembles their lost loved one. Who knows, perhaps if you were just familiar with the case, you would be able to identify one missing persons?

Thanks for purchasing this book, I hope you enjoy it!

Chapter 1: The Leader Went Down

Currently, only one man is assigned to the case of Jimmy Hoffa, but before, more than 200 people were involved in the search of the missing union leader. The years may have already decreased the "appeal" of the case, but for those who lived during the controversy's time, they would never forget the mystery it brought.

Hero or Villain?

Jimmy Hoffa was a renowned union leader of his time. In his twenties, he was already popular with the IBT, or the International Brotherhood of Teamsters. When he became the group's leader, it garnered a total of 1.5 million members, which made it the largest union when it came to the number of members.

Americans of the working class saw him as the hero who brought changes to benefit the laborers. Unknown to them, Jimmy was also an active felon. When he started to become the leader, he committed many crimes, and in the process, acquired many enemies-- especially mafia groups.

One of the enemies Jimmy had made was President Kennedy's brother, Bobby. Since he was "immune" to any arrest in the 50's, Bobby poured time and effort into bringing Jimmy down. When the 60's came, Bobby became the head counsel of Senate Select Committee on Improper Activities in the Labor and Management Field. Afterward, he became an attorney and interrogated Jimmy in the courtroom.

In 1962, Bobby succeeded in finding a fault in the union leader: extortion of illegal payments. However, it turned into a hung jury. Nevertheless, it was found out that Jimmy was trying to bribe one of the jurers, so he was arrested anyway and was sentenced to serve 8 years in prison.

Two years after that, he was proven guilty of embezzling 1.7 million dollars from the pension plan of the union. He could consider himself lucky because his connections prevented him from going to jail, but even legal favors only went so far because in the end, he served almost 5 years in prison.

When Nixon became the president, he freed Jimmy, on one condition-- he needed to stay away from any form of union and politics until the 80's, when his sentence was supposed to end. Jimmy failed to follow this condition, in fact, he became even more aggressive, especially when he found out that his former right hand man, Frank Fitzsimmons, was already the union leader.

For the mob, Frank was easier to manipulate than Jimmy, so they warned Jimmy off from trying to regain leadership. Those warnings, however, fell on Jimmy's deaf ears.

Last seen in Red Fox

On July 30, 1975, the inevitable happened, Jimmy Hoffa suddenly disappeared. Before the disappearance, he received an appealing call to meet up with three powerful people: a mobster, a labor boss from Detroit, and a person with a high position in Teamsters. The supposed rendezvous point was the Red Fox restaurant, just outside Detroit.

He arrived first and entered the restaurant, but after 30 minutes of waiting and no one appearing, he called his wife to tell her that he would wait for a few more minutes and then he would go home. When he left the restaurant, Jimmy was never seen again.

When witnesses were interviewed, they said that Jimmy was last seen leaving with three men and getting inside a car. The FBI concluded that he was killed in the said car, although no further proofs were revealed at that time. Two of the suspected people who met with him were Anthony "Tony" Giacolone and Anthony Provenzano.

According to the FBI, the meeting was supposed to be a

peace treaty, but when Jimmy didn't agree, he was murdered. Despite the claims, Tony had a valid alibi with a lot of witnesses on the day of the disappearance.

When the car where Jimmy was taken to was recovered, they found Jimmy's hair and blood, but other than that, no other leads surfaced. Since Jimmy made a lot of enemies, the list of suspects seemed endless. No one wanted to do anything with the case so the FBI had to hypnotize witnesses. Even with that attempt, clues still proved to be elusive.

There were a lot of theories when it came to the location of the body. Some said that his remains were put in a drum before it was buried in Brother's Moscato Junkyard. Other theorized locations were the football stadium in East Rutherford where the body was suspected to have been mixed with the concrete, the helideck of the Sheraton Savannah Resort Hotel and the garage of the Cadillac, Michigan.

In 2006, Richard Kulinski claimed that he murdered Jimmy using a knife. According to him, he placed the body in a drum, buried it in the junkyard, but when the police investigated the place, he dug it out and transported it to Japan-- where it was used as a scrap metal.

Jimmy was declared legally dead in 1982, but the case is

Missing People

still open up to now.

Chapter 2: Lost in the Indiana Dunes Since 1966

3 girls who only wanted to swim at the beach had gone missing-- could it be foul play? Or did the girls have secrets of their own that drove them to disappear willingly? Surely, if that's the case, they would still return to their families-- so why are they still missing now?

Joining the crowd

On July 2, 1966, 3 friends set out on a simple plan- go to the beach, enjoy it for couple of hours, and return home. Since she was the one who owned a vehicle, a 1955 Buick, Anne Miller who was 21 years old at that time, went out first. She wore a blue two piece bathing suit with a belt.

From her home in West Suburban Lombard, she drove to her friend's house in Suburban Westchester. There, Patricia Blough was waiting. She, too, wore a swimsuit: a two piece with ruffles. Before leaving, she told her mother that she wouldn't be gone for long because their other friend had to be back to prepare her husband's dinner.

From Patricia's house, the two went to pick up their third friend-- 19 year old Renee who wore a bathing suit with golden leaves and green flowers. On their way to the beach, they bought suntan lotion. When they reached Indiana Dunes Park, they joined more than 9000 people, and Ann's vehicle joined 2000 others.

Invited on board

In the beach park, they stayed under a tree approximately 100 yards away from the shore of Lake Michigan. Near them was a couple who was sight-seeing and was guarding their belongings. Walking to the shore were thousands of people. The three friends left together leaving their belongings unattended, so when the day came to an end and they hadn't returned yet, it was the couple who told the ranger that the wallets and blankets belonged to three girls who left presumably to swim.

While doing so, the couple told him that the girls talked to a young, tanned guy on a boat. They last saw the girls when they got on board the boat which was only 14-16 feet long, painted white on the outside, with a blue interior. The ranger thought nothing of it because it was a common occurrence so he simply took the girl's belongings for safekeeping.

Reported missing

After celebrating the 4th of July, the ranger received a call from Patricia's father, telling him that his daughter had not returned home from their trip to the beach. When the ranger inspected the belongings of the three girls, he found a miniature license plate. Searching the parking lot revealed that the same license plate number was on Ann's 1955 Buick. So, were the girls still in the water?

The police became immediately involved in the case. They also found out that Ann's family had already filed a missing persons report. Virtually every corner was searched-- the shorelines, the caves, the woods, the water. A lot of people became involved including scuba divers, cutters, and coast guards. Despite all the efforts though, Ann, Patricia, and Renee were still missing.

Some light was shed when one vacationer offered help in the investigation. On the day the three girls disappeared, he was video-taping the beach. When the police surveyed the footage, two boats fitted the description of the couple, and surprisingly enough, the girls went on board both boats. The first was smaller-- a Tri-hull, and then 3 hours later, they were found boarding the second Trojan Cabin Cruiser along with three other men.

The names of the boats and their owners, however, were not known. According to the police, it would be very difficult to pinpoint the vehicles since there were approximately 5000-6000 boats in the area on that day. Their conclusion was that the girls were just picked up by the smaller boat, but the party was really on the bigger one.

The first theory that the authorities looked into was drowning, however, the girls' family refused to believe it. According to them, all the girls were physically fit and were good swimmers. They could have helped each other, or at least one of them would have been able to survive.

Further investigation

Dick Wylie, a former newsman turned law enforcer believed that the girls' disappearance was premeditated. Wylie has written over 120,000 words in a report about the case. He interviewed a lot of people and had done more investigation than the police. He also delved deeper into the girls' private affairs.

According to him, Patricia had an ex-convict for a boyfriend. When her other friends were interviewed, they said that several months before, Patricia had bruises caused by the boyfriend. The police, however, found nothing to link him to Patricia's or the other two's disappearance. At this point, even the FBI was already involved.

Further investigation by Wylie revealed that both Patricia and Ann had a relationship with married men. When the two got pregnant, they had to resort to abortion to avoid any scandal. Since abortion was illegal in Illinois at that time, the girls employed the services of Frank and Helen Largo.

The Largos were known to run an abortion mill that operated on boats. According to Wylie, the young tanned man the girls talked to was a part of the Largos team. It could be that one of the operations ended up in disaster. To get rid of witnesses and to avoid eyes to turn to their abortion mill, all of the girls were killed.

As for Renee, the only married one among the three, was found that she was also facing problems in her marriage. A letter to her husband was also found. The content of the letter was simple: she wanted a divorce. This prompted others to believe that they really disappeared willingly. For Renee's father, Joseph Slunecko, they must have planned to return after some time, but they were embarrassed since they had already caused a lot of commotion.

Up to now, the girls are still missing. In a desperate attempt to solve the case, the police hired a psychic. Said psychic mentioned that the girls' bodies were in a cabin that could only be seen from the lake.

Although the police found a cabin, no sign of violence was revealed, and not one body was there. With witnesses either dead or having difficulty in remembering, and with no further clues, the case of the Indiana Dunes Women,

Missing People was already over, but still unsolved.

Chapter 3: Friends, Booze, and Phone Calls

How would you feel if, after a short out-of-town journey with your boyfriend, you went home and found your teenage daughter missing?

Judith Rahn was devastated. She had no clue; was her daughter abducted? If so, why? Did she decide to go live on her own? Again, if that was the case, why didn't she just inform her mother?

More than 30 years after the disappearance, Judith and the authorities still don't know what happened on the fateful day of April 26, 1980 – the day Laureen Rahn vanished into thin air.

At Home with Company

It was spring break at Parkside Junior High School, and as such, a lot of students planned on "taking it easy". Many stayed at home, some went on a trip with their family, while the others would hang out with their school friends. Laureen Rahn, one of the students, was supposed to accompany her mother, Judith, and Judith's boyfriend out of town.

Judith's boyfriend was a professional tennis player and on

that day, he had a tournament, so as usual, they asked Laureen to come with them. Laureen, however, declined; she asked Judith if she could just stay home and the mother, thinking nothing of it, agreed.

And so, Laureen stayed at home in their third floor apartment at Merrimack Street in Manchester, New Hampshire. In the evening, a female and a male friend came over; they drank wine and beer. The time when Laureen's male friend left was not mentioned in the reports, but according to him, he heard voices in the hallway, so he left through the backdoor thinking that Judith had returned.

Apparently, he was afraid that he would get in trouble, thus when he heard Laureen locked the door behind him, he fled.

Laureen's female friend, however, slept there.

Mystery in Darkness

When Judith returned home at around midnight, she was shocked that it was so dark. Upon closer inspection, she realized that all the lightbulbs in the hallway – in all three floors of the apartment building – were unscrewed. Furthermore, their apartment door was also unlocked. Feeling weird, but not worried, she went inside and checked on her daughter's room. She thought she found her sleeping there.

However, in the morning, Judith found out that the person in the bed was Laureen's female friend. So she asked where Laureen was, the unnamed friend said that she had last seen her on the couch, sleeping. Looking around the house, Judith said that her daughter's clothes were in the closet, her brand new sneakers were kept, and surprisingly, the back door was open.

Runaway… Or Not?

At first, the authorities believed Laureen to be a typical teenage runaway, but Judith insisted that it was impossible: her clothes were in the apartment, her purse was there, and they had no known problems which may urge the 14-year old to run away from home. The police, after some time, also changed their stance and said that Laureen must have left willingly, but with the intention of returning home.

Only, she didn't. Or she wasn't able to.

Months after Laureen went missing, Judith found out that she was charged for three phone calls to California – calls, which, if her memory served right, she didn't make. For one, she didn't know anyone in California: no friends and absolutely no relatives.

She was also sure that Laureen had no ties whatsoever in

that area. Two of the calls were made from a motel in Santa Monica to another motel in Santa Ana; the third was disturbing: it was to a teen sexual assistance hotline.

The authorities interviewed the physician who was taking care of the calls, but he adamantly denied that he had any connection with the New Hampshire missing teen. That stand held on until 1985.

More to It Than Meets the Eye

In 1985, the same physician changed his story – he said that his wife could have met a young lady from New Hampshire. Allegedly, during those times, a lot of young runaway women would visit their house and talk to his wife. He then directed the authorities to a woman named Annie Sprinkle, a person his wife worked with in the fashion industry. According to the doctor, Annie could know some things about some of the young ladies.

It turned out Ms. Annie Sprinkle was involved in child pornography. The police watched several of her films (it was not mentioned why not all were scanned), but they found nothing that connected to Laureen.

In 1986, an investigator on behalf of Judith visited the two motels involved in the 1980 phone calls; said investigator found out that one of the hotels was linked to a certain Dr. Z, a pornographer. After this, the clues went cold. Neither Dr. Z nor Annie Sprinkle were punished and it was not even known if these two people were connected to each other.

Progressing Mystery and Sightings

Roger Maurais, Laureen's former boyfriend received a call in 1986; according to his mother who picked up the phone, the woman on the other line said she was "Laureen" or "Laurie" and that she was Roger's ex-girlfriend. Up to this day, the identity of the caller remains unknown.

A relative of the family also claimed that someone who matched Laureen's description was seen at a bus terminal in Boston, Massachusetts. Again, this sighting was not confirmed.

Perhaps the most terrifying aspect of this case (second, of course, to the disappearance itself), were the "silent" phone calls that Judith received. According to her report, the phone calls would come at approximately 3:45 am, and each time she answered, the caller would just remain silent.

One time, when it was Laureen's sister who answered the call, the person on the other end simply "listened" before hanging up. For several years, these mysterious calls pursued (especially on Christmas holidays); it only stopped after Judith changed her phone number.

In 1985, the man who was drinking with Laureen on the night she disappeared committed suicide – he was never indicted nor was he even considered a suspect.

In 1988, someone reported seeing a prostitute matching Laureen's description in Anchorage, Alaska, but the authorities believed that it wasn't her since the witness based the looks from Laureen's 1980 photos.

A Web of Disappearances

Judith, perhaps due to the building stress of her daughter's disappearance, moved from New Hampshire to Florida; later on she also remarried. She believes that the three phone calls back in 1980 were placed by Laureen, and that she is still alive somewhere. Judith also suspected that her daughter's friends knew more about the case than they were letting on.

Although a solid connection was not determined, it is worth mentioning that just 6 weeks after Laureen disappeared, Denise Denault, a 26-year old woman who lived just 2 blocks away from the Rahns, also disappeared. The weird thing about it was that Laureen and Denise were known to resemble each other despite the age difference. To make things more complicated, just a month before Laureen went missing, a girl of the same age, named Rachel Garden, also mysteriously vanished. All these three cases were never solved.

In one Reddit post it was mentioned by one jmc1995, that his (or her) mother was the female friend of Laureen's who slept over in their house the night of the disappearance. According to jmc1995, his mother said that they hung out with 2 guys, not just one.

The first guy was 18 years old, and the other was 21. It was the 18-year-old who was working in a store who got them their drinks. His father mentioned that back then, his mom said that perhaps, one of the guys returned to pick up Laureen.

Please note that in some reports, the date of Laureen's disappearance was April 27, 1980.

Chapter 4 : Grabbed from the Cradle

Babies are vulnerable: they can't speak to let adults know what they want, so what they do is cry. When a baby is robbed from his crib while peacefully sleeping, the chances of him crying would be slim. Perhaps that was why the kidnapper took the Lindbergh baby while he was very much sound asleep.

Taken from the crib

On March 1, 1932, a 20-month old baby was taken from his room while sleeping. The said baby was Charles Lindbergh Jr., only son of the aviation hero Charles Lindbergh. Charles Senior became popular when he was able to fly solo over the Atlantic Ocean in 1927. On the fateful day, Charles Jr. was put to sleep in his room at the family's mansion in Hopewell, New Jersey.

At 8:00 pm, the family nurse, Betty Gow placed the baby down in his baby clothes and fastened them with pins before setting him down in his crib. Two hours later, she checked the room and found the crib empty-- the Lindbergh baby was missing.

At first Betty thought that one of the parents took him, so when she saw Mrs. Lindbergh in the bathroom, she asked her if the child was with her or his father. When Mrs. Lindbergh said she didn't take the child, Betty proceeded to ask Charles, and again, was told that he didn't take his son.

This set the whole house into an uproar, with Charles leading the search. He started in the nursery where the baby was last seen and discovered that there was a note from the supposed kidnappers.

A case of kidnapping

The note was badly written, with many wrong spelling and grammatical errors. The gist of the ransom note was for the Lindbergh family to give the kidnapper $50,000 in exchange for the toddler. According to the note, the money should come in small, diverse bills. Below the letter were two interconnected circles-- one blue, and one red. There were also holes outside the circles.

After the note was discovered the New Jersey Police immediately became involved. Searching the house, they found a broken ladder going up to the toddler's room. This prompted them to believe that the kidnapper broke the ladder after going up, before taking the baby, or after going down, when he already had toddler.

There were also muddy footprints in the room, as well as tire prints outside the house. The police, however, was not able to inspect the tire prints further because of the bad weather. Another puzzling fact was the lack of fingerprints in the nursery. Aside from the baby's, no other fingerprints were found-- even Betty Gow's prints were not on the places she had touched.

After that night, the sad news of the kidnapping spread and many people went out of their way to help and offer clues, although none of them became useful. Criminals and felons even offered to assist in finding the missing toddler in exchange for money or legal favors.

When no leads emerged, the FBI joined the police. This was not supposed to be the case because kidnapping wasn't a federal crime, but according to president Hoover himself, heaven and earth would be moved to find Charles Jr.

True enough, almost all got involved in the case, including Customs Services, the Coast Guard, and Immigration Services. They offered $25,000 for whoever could give valid information about the kidnappers, and the Lindberghs offered another $50,000. Three days passed and no sign of the kidnappers appeared, until they received another note with the familiar blue and red circles. The 2nd note said that instead of $50,000, they wanted an additional $20,000 because the family asked for police assistance.

Malcolm Cliver

Jafsie's Help

Out of the blue (or out of the kindness of his heart), John "Jafsie" F. Condon tried to help. Jafsie was a retired teacher and a well-liked person in the Bronx. He offered the kidnapper $1000-- all the abductors needed to do was to hand over the baby to a Catholic priest. The kidnappers read Jafsie's note and decided that he could be an intermediary between them and the Lindbergh family.

Jafsie agreed to do this, to finally end the case. Using a newspaper ad, Jafsie contacted the kidnappers-- the ad said *"Money is ready. Jafsie."* The set up was like this: a representative of the kidnappers would take the money and tell Jafsie where the baby was, the meeting would be held at night, in Woodlawn Cemetery.

On the night of the meeting, the representative arrived but never showed himself, he just stayed in the shadows. He introduced himself as John, a Scandinavian sailor working with three other men and two women. He told Jafsie that the baby was safe in the hands of the women he worked with.

Despite his assurance that the baby was unharmed, he asked Jafsie if he would be punished if the baby was dead. This prompted Jafsie to ask for more proof of the toddler's well-being before setting up another meeting. The representative agreed, so on March 16, 1932, Jafsie received Charles Jr.'s sleeping suit.

Another meeting was scheduled, this time, the intention was to give the whole amount of money raised and have the baby once and for all. Jafsie communicated using the newspaper ad again and told the kidnappers that he would be going alone, just like the last time.

On April 1, Jafsie took the specially prepared money. The box where the money was placed could be traced to the kidnappers. The bills had gold certificates in them so that the perpetrators would attract attention should they use the money. The serial number of each bill was recorded.

A cab driver handed a note to Jafsie: it held the details on where to meet and at what time. When Jafsie arrived, he gave the money, while telling the representative that they were only able to raise $50,000. The kidnapper accepted the money and told Jafsie that Charles Jr. was in a boat named Nellie. The boat could be found near Martha's Vineyard in Massachusetts. According to him 2 women, who were not involved with them, had the toddler.

Jafsie and the authorities searched the specified location, but they failed to see the baby. There was no boat named Nellie and there were no women. More depressing was the fact that on May 12, Charles Jr.'s body was found less than a mile from the Lindbergh Mansion in Hopewell. An autopsy report said that the body was already decomposing.

The cause of death was a blow to the head which caused the baby's skull to fracture. Externally, the baby was attacked by wild animals. From the evidence, it was clear that Charles Lindbergh Jr. was killed on the same night he disappeared. The Lindberghs then decided to cremate the body and donate their home to a charitable institution.

What really happened?

The death of the toddler only sparked various theories about who the kidnappers really were. What would drive them to kill the baby with a blow to the head? These, along with all the other questions remained unanswered until September of 1934 when a marked ransom bill was spotted. The marked money was paid by a driver at a gasoline station. The gasoline boy thought the man was suspicious, so what he did was note down the license plate on the bill and called the police.

The plate led them to Bruno Hauptmann, a German national who had criminal records in his home country. He was found with a $20 marked bill, and when his home was searched, more than $14,000 of marked money was recovered. When asked, Bruno Hauptmann said a friend of his gave it to him. Shortly after that, more evidence emerged against Hauptmann when the police saw a note with Jafsie's contact details.

Although he told the police that he put it there "just in case", what got their attention was the similarity of the handwriting to the ones on the ransom notes. When his attic was searched, the police found wood which was the same of the ladder found in the Lindbergh home. Hauptmann was tried and was charged guilty of 1st degree murder. He was electrocuted on April 3, 1936 in New Jersey State Prison.

One could argue that the case suddenly became too easy after finding Hauptmann; so many theorists said that the police (or another group) must have intentionally framed him. Many loose ends were still there: the calmness of Charles Sr., his connection to the mob, why the police allowed the civilians in the crime scene, and the lack of the fingerprints.

For some, the kidnapping was an inside job. Someone knew the goings on in the mansion for him to know the exact time to take the baby. One of the suspects was Violet Sharpe, who was the housekeeper of the family. Although she provided a good alibi, her statements varied each time she was questioned. She also looked nervous whenever she talked to the police. Before the final questioning, Violet committed suicide.

Others even questioned Jafsie. Why did he volunteer to partake in the investigation when he didn't know the family personally? Some even pointed out that the name of the kidnapper was same as his-- John. On top of that, he never gave the baby's sleeping suit to the police, when it could have given further clues.

Even though one man was executed for the kidnapping and murder, some people believed that he was innocent. Perhaps someone used him as a scape goat and whoever was responsible was never punished.

Chapter 5: Like Mother, Like Daughter

Annette Sagers' story is brief but is certainly unique, and of course, creepy. According to reports, Annette, a 12-year old girl went missing from the same spot where her mother also mysteriously vanished. Hence, let us first hear the story of Korrina Lynne Sagers Malinoski.

Missing Mother

5 days before Thanksgiving, on November 20, 1987, Korrina Lynne Sagers Malinoski went out to drive toward Highway 52 in Mount Holly, South Carolina with the known intention of returning home; after all, she was married and had one biological daughter to take care of.

At around 11:00 pm to 11:30 pm, she was last seen leaving Mount Holly Plantation where she and her family resided in the caretaker's house (her husband was the caretaker of the plantation).

When morning came, Korrina's boss at the convenience store where she worked at in Summerville wondered why she hadn't shown up for work. Eager to find out if something was wrong, the boss came looking for her and found Korrina's car parked and locked in front of the Mount Holly Plantation.

The husband, Steven Malinoski was interviewed and he relayed the same information: Korrina went out for a drive and didn't return. The authorities started an extensive search effort both by land and air, but to no avail. Korrina's parents in Iowa were also asked if they knew anything, but they didn't.

Since then, nothing was heard from Korrina until October 4, 1988, when her daughter, Annette Deanne Sagers also vanished.

On the Same Spot

At 7:00 am on October 4, 1988, Annette stood at the bus stop in front of the Mount Holly Plantation; her bus would soon arrive to send her to Westview Middle School where she already was a sixth grader. However, when the bus arrived at 7:20 am, Annette was nowhere to be found.

Her stepfather, Steven, didn't notice that she was missing until that afternoon, when Annette failed to return home and he discovered that she didn't reach her school in the first place.

It was Steven who called the police this time.

Chief L. Randy Herod of the Barkeley County Sheriff's Office still remembered that moment when Steven made the report. Voice strained, he said that Annette failed to go to school and that she hadn't come back home yet.

Missing People

Just like how it was nearly a year before, the authorities performed an extensive search, interviewed Steven, asked the public for help, and informed Korrina's parents, but again, their efforts bore no fruit.

The highlight of the case was the note found at the narrow shelter of the bus stop. The paper was clearly from a notebook and the letter was scrawled using a pencil; it said: "Dad, momma came back. Give the boys a hug."

The content of the note suggests that Annette wrote it for Steve, who had two boys safe at home. Handwriting experts, upon investigation, determined that the note was truly from Annette.

Theories

Despite the fact that the note really came from Annette, a lot of people still believe that she could have been under duress when she wrote it. Perhaps the one responsible for Korrina's disappearance found out that Annette knew something, and in an effort to escape the law, he or she also removed Annette from the equation.

On the other side, some people believe that Korrina really went back for her daughter. They suspect that Steven, the husband, was abusive towards her, so she fled, took a year to build a new life, and came back for Annette in the fear that Steven would also hurt her.

Malcolm Cliver

In 2000, an anonymous call was placed telling the police to look for a corpse in Sumter County; cadaver-sniffing dogs were sent together with the searchers, but they found no corpse.

To date, both cases are still unsolved, but the authorities have already ruled out family abduction as there was no evidence to suggest otherwise. Despite this, a lot of enthusiasts wonder if Steven was interviewed as extensively as she should have been.

Chapter 6 : Where is Zebb?

While others who disappeared were celebrities or known personalities, Zebb Quinn was just the typical guy next door, so what could have caused his disappearance?

Car hunting

Zebb worked in Wal-Mart in North Carolina, more specifically the branch on Hendersonville Road, Ashville. On January 2, 2000, after finishing his shift, he and his friend and co-worker Robert Owens, met in the store's parking lot. They planned on visiting a Mitsubishi dealership because Zebb had seen a car he wanted to buy there.

From the store, they drove their own cars and went to a gas station to buy sodas. On the security camera, they were seen at around 9:15 pm before heading out to Long Shoals road.

When they neared T.C. Robertson High School, Zebb signaled Robert to pull over. He told Robert that he received a page and would have to use a phone. 10 minutes later, Zebb returned looking distressed and told him that he couldn't go on with the plan to look for cars. He left Robert and was never again seen.

The Suspects

Several hours after they parted, Robert was admitted to a hospital due to a head injury from a traffic accident. The police found it odd because no vehicular accident report was filed under his name. What was weirder was when Robert called the next morning asking for sick leave-- he did this while pretending to be Zebb. Trouble was, the one who received the call knew Zebb's voice, so he was caught. When Robert was questioned about it, he just said that Zebb asked him to do it. Other than that, he refused to cooperate.

Other people were also interviewed, including the girl Zebb was seeing. Apparently, the girl, Misty, also had a boyfriend. The boyfriend in question was, according to Zebb's account to his other friends, violent. The two denied any connection with Zebb's disappearance.

Zebb's pager was also examined. When they checked the message that made him anxious, they found out that it came from his Aunt, Ina Ustich. Ina denied that she sent the message, she even told the police that she had witnesses: Misty, her mother (which was Ina's friend), and Misty's boyfriend.

Two weeks after Zebb disappeared, his car was found near the hospital where his mother worked. Inside it was a Labrador puppy, a drawn pair of lips on the windshield, bottles, jacket, and hair, but none of them belonged to

Missing People

Zebb. There was also a hotel key card, but the police was not able to trace what hotel it belonged to. None of them produced new leads. Zebb's mother believed that someone intentionally placed the car there, someone who knew she worked there.

Zebb's family believed that Misty, her boyfriend, and Ina were involved in his disappearance, but there was no evidence to arrest them. Robert was not charged with anything involving Zebb's case, but he served time in prison for various crimes. In 2015 he was arrested for murders and the disappearance of a couple who hired him to do some construction jobs. Up to now, Zebb's case is still open.

Chapter 7: Missing Photos

Being a photojournalist can be exciting – you get to go to places that some people can only dream of, you can immortalize a moment with just a click, and most importantly, if your shot turns out to be memorable, you can become a part of history.

What most people don't know, however, is the fact that photojournalism has its danger, especially if you are assigned to cover calamities like hurricanes, or tragedies like war.

Sean Flynn, son of Hollywood's esteemed, Errol Flynn *(The Adventures of Robin Hood, 1938)*, was in Cambodia in April 6, 1970. He was only 28 years old, but was already selected to join the valued team of *Time Magazine* reporters who covered the Second World War in Cambodia. On that day, together with 31-year-old Dana Stone, Sean rode his motorbike toward the position of the guerillas.

He never returned. Neither did Dana Stone.

Grief of Teammates

Finding no closure was hard, not just for Dana's and Sean's family and friends, but also to those people who worked alongside them during wartime. Tim Page, a British photographer who was also part of the team survived the war (albeit, barely), but not the mystery of the disappearance.

Now, more than 40 years after the vanishing, he is still looking for answers. According to Mr. Page, it was even harder to let go because it was like not being able to bring your mates home from war. According to him, the last time he had seen Sean was in a hospital in Saigon where he had been confined after being involved in a landmine blast which almost killed him and rendered him temporarily blind.

Sean was in Laos at the time of the blasting, but immediately after he heard of Mr. Page's involvement, he took the next flight to Saigon. "He was standing there in a white Pakistani wedding shirt," Mr. Page related of his last memory of Sean at the hospital.

True, a lot of journalists were killed during war, some of them also went missing, but since Sean had a strong presence (on top of being a son of famous actor), his and Dana's disappearance marked the press community. Many of them expected the duo to pop out of nowhere with big stories about their journey, but after years of cold tracks, it became apparent that that would no longer happen.

Malcolm Cliver

Adventurous by Nature

Unknown to some people, Sean Flynn was an actor himself: he was first seen in his father's television show, *The Errol Flynn Theater* at the age of 15. In 1961, at the age of 20, he signed a contract to play the lead role in *The Son of Captain Blood*, a sequel to one of his father's movies, *Captain Blood*.

Despite the fact that he had a lot of potential to be as famous as his father on the big screen, Sean obviously got bored with filming. So, in 1964, he went to Africa and became a safari guide and big-game hunter. When he went to Kenya, he worked as a game warden.

However, being adventurous also sometimes meant no money, so in the later part of 1965, Sean starred again in two Italian Westerns and in the summer of 1966, he flew to Singapore to shoot his last movie, *Five Ashore in Singapore*. This happened even though in January of the same year, he already had found his true calling: photojournalism.

He first worked for *Paris Match*, then transferred to *Time Life* and *United Press International*. In no time, Sean, along with others like Dana Stone, Tim Page, and Nik Wheeler made a name for himself; his photos reached people all over the globe and became known as one of those high-risk photojournalists who would do anything for a great shot.

In his "adventures" as a photojournalist, Sean already suffered a wounded knee, made a parachute jump with the 101st Airborne Division, and covered the Arab-Israeli War. He even planned on creating a documentary about the war; unfortunately, he didn't return to bring this mission to life.

Unclear Fate

On that tragic date of April 6, 1970, Sean's team had just left Phnom Penh to attend a press conference in Saigon, now Ho Chi Minh City. Unlike the others who rode in limousines, he and Dana (who worked for CBS News) chose to ride their motorbikes. After the conference, they heard a lead which said that the Viet Cong (Vietnam Communist Soldiers) were guarding a checkpoint on Highway 1 in Cambodia. Hence, alone on their motorbikes, they sped off the Highway and were never seen again.

It was never confirmed, but *Time* speculated that the duo was captured by the Viet Cong, held captive for 1 year, and were killed by the Khmer Rouge, the Cambodian Communist Organization. This claim, however, emanates doubt since no remains were ever recovered.

Sean's mother and Errol's first wife, Lily Damita, spent an

normous amount of fortune to search for her missing son until 1984 when she had him declared as legally dead. 10 years later, perhaps of exhaustion, loss of hope, and a broken heart, she also died.

Memories from the Past

Lilly collected everything about her son, and this is mainly the reason why the world now can appreciate the vanished (and perhaps, long-dead) photojournalist. In his letters and early photos, it was apparent that Sean would rather have his own way than gain the approval of those around him, his father included. One such letter said: "If Father and M.G.M. want me to do a picture, they can all go to hell…"

In another sincere but haunting note, Sean expressed his love for Lilly. He thanked her for the home and the car and for the fact that she was the best mother he could ever want. He related that he tried to be with her as much as possible, but situations hindered it. "Although you never hear me say it, I love you very much!" – one line in the letter said.

Perhaps, the saddest part of Sean's disappearance was the fact that no one could investigate what happened – it was wartime after all and anything could have happened. No talk about the photoshoot they had with the Viet Cong; it wasn't even clear if they reached their destination.

Missing People

If some people witnessed what became of them, no one uttered a word and perhaps no one would – chances are, those witnesses died with them or died of old age. The only hope is for a written account from someone, and no one knows for sure if one will ever turn up.

People like Tim Page, who is now 69, will probably never stop looking – not when he still holds on to the hope that Sean's fate may surface along with the photos he risked his life to take.

Chapter 8 - Soaring Away

The sky is as dangerous as the land or water. As much as you can get lost in the ocean and land terrain, the whole sky can also take you away and never bring you back. Today's technology definitely makes us safer, but the fact that most people try to dismiss is, technology can also hide some crimes. Because really, how can a plane disappear in the sky and not have anyone figure out where it is?

Lost in the Sky

From the Kuala Lumpur International Airport in Malaysia, Flight 370, was suppose to travel towards Beijing Capital International Airport in China. On March 8, 2014, Flight 370, which was a Boeing 777 plane, took off. In the plane were 239 passengers and twelve crew members. Nearly an hour after it took off, just as it crossed the South China Sea, a voice contact from the Boeing 777 was initiated in Air Traffic Control.

A few minutes after the attempted contact, the plane disappeared from the traffic radar. Good thing the Malaysian Military radar was still able to follow its course. According to their records, Flight 370 changed its planned path: it crossed the Malay Peninsula. Another hour went by and the plane was spotted over Adaman Sea.

After that, the military radar also lost the plane. When the Satellite Communications Analysis was pulled out, it was revealed that the plane still travelled for 7-8 hours until it reached the Indian Ocean.

The Information, or the lack thereof

And that was exactly what the government reported to the public. On March 20, the Malaysian Government stated that the Boeing 777 ended its course in the Indian Ocean. The investigation was still open. No more details were provided-- nothing about the remains of the plane were discussed, and no information about the passengers and crew were disclosed.

This made the public both disappointed and suspicious. Friends and family of the crew and passengers gathered outside the Malaysian Embassy to make them disclose any information about the whereabouts of their loved ones. Their approach proved to be unsuccessful.

The lack of details led many to make their own theories about what happened to the Boeing 777.

Theories

It crashed in the Indian Ocean. Since all the government said was the plane's course ended in it, a lot of people immediately thought that the plane crashed there.

However, experts said that it was impossible. Since the plane was a Boeing 777, it wouldn't be able to withstand such a crash. Crashing in the Indian Ocean would be synonymous to someone crashing into a cemented surface at a very high speed.

The plane would have been torn to millions of pieces. If that was the case, there would be a lot of evidence. Soft objects like cushions would float, and some pieces of the plane would be washed ashore. In other words, it would be a very obvious accident and no more questions about "disappearance" would emerge. Crashing would also be highly unlikely because no distress signal was sent by the plane. So yes, this theory was rejected right away.

Cockpit fire. More plausible than the crashing theory was the cockpit fire theory. If the cockpit was on fire, the crew would want an emergency landing to the nearest air strip which was located in Palau Langkawi. This would explain the need to change the planned course.

Instead of sending distress signals, the pilot and the crew could have focused more on making sure that the plane would land safely. While on the way to the air strip, the crew might have inhaled smoke and lost consciousness. This would explain why the Boeing 777 still flew for several hours. The problem with this theory was the lack of evidence, and of course, the whereabouts of the plane.

Missing People

It was hijacked. When a plane goes missing, this would be a common theory. One form of hijacking is electronic hijacking, and this is one of the most looked into angles in the Flight 370 disappearance. According to reports, the Boeing 777 had the Boeing Honeywell Uninterrupted Autopilot system. Using this autopilot system, the authority to run and land the plane would be transferred to a navigational computer because the system would remove all the electricity in the vessel.

This was invented to make sure that in case of human hijacking, the pilot won't be commanded as to how to run the plane. It would also be useful in case a pilot becomes incapacitated. In the case of Flight 370, it could be that the system computer was hijacked. This theory was stated by the former Malaysian Prime Minister, Mahathir Mohamad.

Another variation of the above theory was created by Jeff Wise, a technology writer. According to him, it was possible that the hijackers on the plane were able to locate where the electronic bay was (electronic bay was the place where the computer system was installed). From there, they navigated the plane and were sending false signals to all the radars. So, when the radar noted that the plane was travelling south, it could have really gone north to Kazakhstan.

Could it be possible for some people to hijack a plane even when they were not on board? According to other theorists, it was possible-- after all, the plane could be operated using the autopilot system. So, if a person (or a group of people) cyber-attacked the plane, they would be able to change the plane's direction, altitude, and speed. This theory, however, was ruled out.

And finally, the simplest explanation regarding hijacking: terrorist attack. Some theorists, suggested that the Boeing 777 was attacked by the Jihads. The terrorists on the plane could have forced the pilot and the crew to land the plane to either Afghanistan or Pakistan. As for the Jihads' goal, it could be anyone's guess.

The most obvious goal would be to create trouble for the United States or China, but this was disputed because, if that was what they wanted, they should have landed the plane in Diego Garcia where Khalid Sheikh Mohammed, a terrorist, was detained. There were also many American military activities happening in Diego Garcia, so it was a logical choice. Again, this theory lacked evidence.

Aside from crashing, cockpit fire, and hijacking, one angle looked at before was a *patent war*. According to several reports, 4 of the passengers in the plane were inventors of the US 8671381 B1 (a system for optimizing the number of dies on a wafer), the 5th inventor was not on board.

Missing People

Apparently, each inventor held 20% of the shares, so the 4 inventors in the plane had 80% of the shares altogether.

Some suggested that the 5th inventor, Freescale Semiconductor, initiated the plane to disappear to be able to obtain all the shares. However, this was rejected as soon as they found out that even though the 4 inventors were killed, the shares wouldn't be transferred to Freescale Semiconductors.

Further investigation revealed that 22 passengers of the plane were employees of Freescale. They carried with them classified patents. Could it be that the plane was staged to disappear to get rid of the possible patents?

Was the American Government involved? Could it be a conspiracy? Some believed that the plane landed in Diego Garcia where an American Military base is located. How it landed there was unclear-- maybe someone hijacked the plane and forced into that direction, or it was the pilot himself who directed the plane to the base.

The latter sounded more plausible after some records were pulled out. When the authorities inspected the pilot's flight simulator on his home computer, they noticed that the pilot was practicing his skills on how to land a plane on a short runway in the Indian Ocean. However, the FBI stepped down saying that that information was not proven.

A plane captain in France said that it was possible for the American Government to control the plane if it went near their Diego Garcia base. In fact, some witnesses reported that they saw the Boeing 777 "flying too low" on that date.

From the American Government, the attention of some theorists shifted, again, to *Zaharie Ahmad Shah*, the pilot of Flight 370. According to them, the pilot hijacked the plane by himself. This was because of the pilot's strangeness before the flight. It was noted that he made no plans after March 8, neither professional nor personal. Further digging suggested that his marriage was on the rocks-- in fact, on March 7, his wife and three children moved to another home.

And the weirdest bit of information was the phone call received by the pilot a few moments before the Boeing 777 disappeared. The call was clearly from a woman, but the phone number was from an unidentified person. They couldn't be sure who the woman was because the name used to purchase the number was fraudulent. What more, when the FBI restored the deleted info from the pilot's flight simulator, they confirmed that the pilot was indeed practicing how to land on a short runway.

Was it intentional?

Missing People

When the Malaysian Airlines Flight 17 crashed in Ukraine in the same year, reporters concluded that it could be the missing Flight 370. When the authorities inspected, they immediately rejected the idea because it simply meant that the airlines had two identical planes. However, when AirAsia Flight 8501 crashed on December 28, many people suspected that these planes were crashed intentionally.

Did you know that before that, a Chinese internet user "warned" the public about boarding Malaysian planes? In his post he said that people shouldn't fly in Malaysian planes from December 15-17. Either he was just riding the hype of the plane crashes, he was a hacker who came across secret information, or he had knowledge coming from intelligence units of the Chinese Government.

One thing is clear though, as long as the involved authorities withhold information about the plane, people will continue to theorize about what happened. People even thought of the song *"Get It Started"* by Shakira and Pitbull ; in the lyrics of the song, something was mentioned about *"now it's off to Malaysia"*.

The part *"two passports"* was also linked to the two passengers with stolen passports, and lastly, *"three cities, two countries, one day"* got them thinking that it talks about the Flight 370's journey. Who knows?

Chapter 9: Lost Lyricist

Richey Edwards, a Native of Blackwood, Caerphilly Wales was an intelligent man. It was obvious not just in his scholastic records, but also in the lyrics of the songs which his former band, Manic Street Preachers had brought to life. From Oakdale Comprehensive School, he was able to enter and graduate at the University of Wales, Swansea with a degree in Political History.

His inclination in politics radiated in the lyrics of the band's songs – in fact, the lyrics, along with his personality and the way he dressed up secured his "occult" status.

Less Melody, More Words

Originally a driver and a roadie (someone employed to maintain the band's equipment), Richey Edwards – called by those close to him in the band as Richey James – showed little musical talent. From playing the guitar, he later on concentrated on the band's lyrics and design, which according to the rest of the members, honed their musical sound and direction. Before long, Richey became their 4th member and due to his strong (albeit, a little strange) personality, their spokesperson.

On May 15, 1991, a journalist from NME, Steve Lamacq,

questioned not just the band's value's and authenticity, but also Richey's dedication to his art; perhaps both insulted and eager to demonstrate his dedication, Richey responded by taking a blade and carving the words "4 Real" into his left forearm. He needed 18 stitches after that.

His Openness in Depression

In his interviews, Richey became very open about his bouts of depression and its connection to his dressing up. According to him, when he was a child, he wanted people's attention, so he would do his best to dress up.

Now, doing self-harm was a different issue. It was not confirmed if he did it for attention or as his form of expression, but a lot of reports said that Richey did it mainly to rid himself of the pain. "When I feel the pain, I feel nothing else," he said in one interview.

Does that mean he was sick in the mind and he needed help? No one could tell for sure, but Richey himself visited a psychiatric institution, rendering himself unavailable for some of the band's promotional tours.

His last tour with the band was at London Astoria in 1994, where after the live show, all of them smashed their musical instruments.

Malcolm Cliver

Mysterious Disappearance

Some people said that when Richey disappeared on February 1, 1995, it was a planned act. According to records, two weeks before their supposed flight to the US for a promotional tour, he withdrew £200 from his bank account – daily. When February 1 – the schedule of the flight – came, he had withdrawn a total of £2800.

What he used the money for, no one knew, for Richey disappeared and never boarded the plane. What the authorities know is that he checked out of the Embassy Hotel at 7:00 am before visiting his own home at Cardiff, Wales. On February 7, a cab driver from Newport claimed that he picked Richey up from King's Hotel and drove him around the valleys, including Blackwood, which was his hometown.

After the "tour", the taxi driver dropped Richey at Severn View Station and he was paid £68 in cash. The following week after February 7, Richey was seen at the Newport Passport Office and Newport Bus Station; what he did there was anyone's guess.

The Last of Richey

On Valentine's Day, Richey's vehicle – a Vauxhall Cavalier – received a parking ticket at the Severn View Service Station; by February 17, it was already declared abandoned. Close inspection of the vehicle drove the police to suspect that it had been lived in; they also discovered that it had a flat battery.

Could Richey have been suffering problems which he thought no one could help him with? Severn View Service was near the Severn Bridge, which according to locals, was a popular suicide spot. What with his dressing up, depression, and meaningfully haunting words, it was impossible for some people to not assume that he killed himself by jumping from the bridge.

But that theory, according to those closest to Richey, was unlikely. The lyricist – as strange as he was – was strong enough to have the will to live. And true enough, one interview of Richey's clearly said that he was a weak man, but the thought of killing himself never reached his mind because he was "stronger than that".

If he wasn't dead, then where is Richey? Is he still alive? The years following the vanishing was difficult, because of the lack of clues and the abundance of sightings. First, some said he was spotted in Goa, India, then in the islands of Lanzarote and Fuerteventura; none of these sighting were confirmed – none were conclusive.

Lashing Out on the Authorities

Did the police do their best? A lot of people, especially

those close to Richey, said that they didn't. In fact, for them, their efforts were "far from satisfactory". In his book entitled *Everything (A Book About Manic Street Preachers),* Simon Price, a British music journalist, said that the police might have failed in considering Richey's mental state, and so, they failed to prioritize his case.

The family, particularly Richey's younger sister, Rachel, was also frustrated; in fact, Rachel had a "hit out after a police handling" while they were analyzing CCTV footage 2 years after her brother went missing. Simon said that one of the members of the investigation team said that: "the idea of identifying somebody in that (referring to the footage) is arrant nonsense."

The family could have declared Richey dead in 2002, but they refused, holding onto hope as long as they could, but in 2008 Richey Edwards became officially presumed dead.

His Sister's Search and Suspicion

February 1, 2016 marked the 20th anniversary of Richey's disappearance. His sister, Rachel Elias, spoke about many things, including the gruesome search process her family had to go through year after year and how she suspected that Richey already knew that the band's gig at London, Astoria would be his last.

Missing People

The family's main source of information was the Unidentified Database of the UK Missing Persons website. It contains more than 1000 pictures of unidentified bodies and body parts. Some show the remarkable tattoos, and others feature items which could be memorable to someone.

Rachel called some of the pictures as shocking – and so, it wasn't easy for her family to go through the images monthly in the hope that Richey or a part of him, would show up on the website. That would mean he was dead, but that would be significantly better than not having any closure.

As what was mentioned earlier, Richey visited a psychiatric institution before he disappeared. Rachel said it was because of his mixed problems in depression, alcoholism, self-harming, and anorexia. After releasing himself from the hospital, his band-mates said that Richey appeared to be more peaceful, that he developed a certain level of serenity in his aura.

His sister believed that it was because Richey had already determined the course he wanted to take; furthermore, she believed that her brother sent him subtle messages concerning his then future disappearance.

Before Christmas of 1994, Richey took the effort to buy

presents for his loved ones – he even sent gifts to some of his friends at the University. At one point, he talked to everyone seriously, asking them to attend to one of the band's shows in London Astoria. Rachel said he rarely did that; Richey didn't normally encourage his loved ones to watch their gigs, but on his last performance, he sought them out and encouraged them to watch.

To Rachel, it was a premonition of some sort; she felt like her brother had reached a decision. Whatever the decision was, they didn't know. Did he decide to live somewhere else, as a different person? Did he just plan on having a break with the intention to return, but somewhere along met with foul play? Did he decide to kill himself? Rachel could only wish she knew.

Clarifications

When Richey disappeared, he became some sort of legend, but not in an appealing way. He turned into the model of a tortured yet cool hero, and due to that, a lot of depressives, anorexics, self-mutilators, and alcoholics "copied" some of his actions.

Rachel wanted to change that. She felt as if her brother no longer had the personality he truly owned; instead, he became the embodiment of what others wanted to see: a tortured rock n' roll artist. She clarified, that despite the dressing up, the haunting lyrics, and the tortured persona,

Missing People

Richey was cherished and loved by his friends and family. Rachel wanted people to remember the man her brother was, not the myth the others forced out of his vanishing. "He was an intelligent, sensitive man," she added.

Rachel also wanted to clarify something about Richey's self-mutilation – it wasn't as "violent" as the carving of the "4 Real" words. Apparently, in one of the band's shows in Thailand, a fan threw a knife on stage with a note saying: "Cut yourself for me." Richey told his sister that he was appalled by it, and that "it was a shit thing to be remembered for".

Perhaps, the only motivation Richey had when he carved the words on his arm was his need to prove his dedication to his art, but when not provoked, his self-harming only composed of stubbing his skin with cigarettes.

Whatever happened to Richey, no one probably knows. Perhaps he planned to take a vacation; after all, he withdrew a total of £2800 before he went missing. Or maybe, he planned on using that money on the tour itself? Despite the lack of progress, it's still pleasant to know that Richey had been immortalized with the lyrics of the band's songs.

Malcolm Cliver

Chapter 10 : The Missing Film

Definitely underrated, Louis Le Prince was known as the un-awarded pioneer of cinematography. In 1891, Thomas Edison was granted patent for the first ever kinetograph or a motion picture camera. In 1894, Louis and Aguste Lumière from France were recognized for their cinematograph.

Truthfully, the ending decade of the 19th century was full of acknowledgement for different inventors. However, one man was left unrecognized even though he already filmed the first motion pictures way before Edison and the Lumières did. That man was Louis Le Prince.

His world in motion pictures

Louis Aimé Augustin Le Prince is now recognized as the first man to ever shoot a motion picture, but his recognition was not achieved with breeze. In fact, it was clouded with the mystery of his disappearance. Le Prince moved to America from France in the year 1881, but even before transferring, he had already started with his experiments in cinematography, motion pictures, and film stock.

When he moved to America, he simply continued his work until he was able to patent his first invention: a camera with 16 lenses. A huge part of the camera was unsuccessful-- sure, it was able to capture motion, but the images were messy because many lenses were taking pictures at different viewpoints. Nevertheless, he was still recognized for this invention.

His success came in the year 1888. In that year, he went to Leeds, Yorkshire and taped a video he named as *Traffic in the Leeds Bridge*. After that, he also shot another motion picture entitled *Roundhay Garden Scene*. The first video was made on October 1888, a few months after he had already completed his invention. And in the garden scene, he shared his success with his family by casting them in the video.

Due to his invention's success, Le Prince planned to return to London to have it patented, afterwards he would go to America to promote his product. But before all that, he wanted to see his friends and family first. From Bourges, he travelled to Dijon to see his brother. After that his other friends in Paris also expected a visit from him. Le Prince told them that he would arrive on September 16 train.

Imagine their confusion when the Dijon-Paris train arrived on September 16 and Le Prince wasn't on it. He wasn't on the train, and neither was his luggage-- this led many to believe that he didn't even get on board. The last time others saw him was on the platform at Dijon station. From the train, authorities searched the Dijon-Paris railway for him, but also to no avail. From this point on, Louis Le Prince was no longer seen.

Friends, family, and authorities could only have educated theories.

Theories

Could it be suicide? According to Le Prince's brother's grandson, Le Prince could have killed himself. The cause was probably because Le Prince was broke. The grandson concluded that Le Prince took care of everything, that's why no trace of his body and his belongings were seen. Georges Potonniée, a historian, refused believing this notion. According to him, Le Prince knew that his motion picture invention could bring him fortune-- so why would he kill himself?

Could it be Edison's doing? It was very clear that the supposed success of Le Prince could ruin Edison. This made Lizzy, Le Prince's wife, to believe that Edison sent some people to "take care" of his husband. He wanted to prevent the invention from being patented in England, and in the process, he got rid of Le Prince as well.

This notion was not proven. Amidst all these, Equity 6928 was put forth- this would give Le Prince the recognition he deserved. To complete this, Adolphe, Le Prince's son, was summoned to testify. It was only fitting because he helped his father build the invention. The bad news was, Adolphe died while duck hunting in Fire Island, New York two years after the investigation started. This was also linked to Edison, but again, nothing was proven.

Could it be the doing of his family? Pierre Gras, a library director in Dijon, showed some notes to a journalist named Léo Sauvage. In the notes, it was mentioned that Le Prince's family ordered him to disappear because he was a homosexual. The note also said something about Le Prince dying in Chicago in the year 1898. Please take note that Le Prince's homosexuality was not confirmed.

Could it be his brother? Looking back, the last place Le Prince visited was his brother's place in Dijon. That meant that it was his brother who last saw him. By virtue of logic, it could be concluded that he was the one responsible for his disappearance. If he noticed that Le Prince was not right in mind or body, he could have stopped him from leaving. On the other hand, let us not forget that some witnesses reported seeing Le Prince on the platform in Dijon station.

Case Closed

After these, no leads, and no clues to at least shed some

light emerged. From there, Le Prince's case slowly died. The case only gained another spark in 2003 when a photo surfaced. The picture contained a drowning man who had some semblance with Le Prince.

A movie director, David Wilkinson, did a thorough investigation about Le Prince. From his early beginnings to his success in motion picture, he documented as much as he could. He named the documentary, *The First Film*. He offered it to various channels, including BBC and Yorkshire Television in the 1990's, but his offer was refused.

For them, the general public did not know Le Prince all that much to care. However, in the eyes of many historians, directors, and artists, Louis Le Prince was the father of motion pictures.

Chapter 11: Gone in April

April Fabb was born on April 22, 1955; she was a Native of Metton Norfolk. Before her disappearance, she lived at 3 Council Houses with Ernest, her father, her mother, Olive, and an older sister. She had another older sister, but at the time April went missing, that sister was already living with her husband on Cromer Road in Roughton.

Their life was simple until April 8, 1969 when she disappeared, much to her family's horror. What happened to the girl who interestingly vanished in the month where she was named after?

The Timeline

It was around 1:40 pm on April 8, 1969 when April drove her bicycle towards Roughton to visit her sister; she had 10 packets of cigarette, a handkerchief, and $5.50 all contained in a saddle bag. The packets of cigarettes were a gift for her brother in law for his birthday. April was last seen wearing a green jumper, wine-colored skirt, long white socks, and sandals with brass buckles, red straps, and wooden soles.

When she reached Cromer Road, she saw two friends at "Donkey's Field" next to Harrison's Farm and chatted with them for about 10 minutes before finally saying that she was on her way to visit her sister. A little after 2:00

pm, she was well on her way again and an employee at the Harrison's Farm even saw her cycling – it was the last known sighting of April Fabb.

At 2;15 PM, the workers from Ordinance Survey spotted April's bike in a field which was roughly just a few hundred yards away from where she was last seen; no one saw anything suspicious, so the abandoned bicycle didn't make a commotion. However, if April was already missing at that time, then it only means that she vanished in a span of less than 10 minutes.

At 3:00 PM, a civilian man was driving along the area, intent on bringing his mother home, when he saw the abandoned bike at the same spot. Perhaps thinking that the owner just accidentally left it there, he took the bicycle to the Police House in Roughton. The authorities noted that the pack of cigarettes, handkerchief, and money were still in the saddle bag.

Nothing notable happened in the next few hours until the evening came when Olive, April's mother, learned that her daughter was not able to visit her sister in Roughton. The next day, the search and the inquiry began.

The 2-3-mile radius from the field where her bike was found, was searched by the authorities and volunteers, but there was no sign of the 13-year old. A total of 419 houses were visited by the police to conduct an extensive

Missing People

inquiry – many of them were April's family's friends and relatives. However, despite the intensiveness of the search, April's whereabouts remained unknown; her fate, of course, was unclear.

Unsolved but Not Forgotten

It's been 45 years but some people will not lose hope; true, April's mother had died in 2013 and her father had long since passed in 1998 – both not knowing what happened to their daughter – but the family and some of the constabularies think that it's high time for the investigation to be opened again.

One of those who agree is Chris Clark, a former Police Constabulary in King's Lynn Division; according to him, there are some things in the case that were not given enough attention, like the possible involvement of famed child murderer Robert Black.

Back then, Black was already treated as a possible suspect, but the police were skeptical since he was not from around the area (he was residing at King's Cross); it then meant that he must have driven his way to Roughton. However, the authorities argued that he didn't get a license until 1976.

April's surviving sister, Diane Field said that she always thought that Black could somehow be connected because even back then, people could and would drive without a license. Asked if she was okay with reopening the case, she said that she would welcome it.

If you'll look closely at Black's crimes, you can see some similarities to April's case. First, he concentrated on young girls: Jennifer Cardy, for an instance, was abducted and killed just two weeks after her 9th birthday. Her body was recovered a mile away from their home in County Antrim 6 days after she went missing.

Susan Maxwell was 11 years old, and Caroline Hogg was just 5. He was also confirmed responsible for the disappearance of 13-year-old Genette Tate, but before he could be officially charged with it, he died in January of 2016. Both Genette and Jennifer – like April – were riding their bicycles when Black approached them.

But that wasn't just Mr. Clark's basis; according to him, reports of a red Mini were seen around the area when April disappeared. The vehicle had a reflective plate which would only come to force four years later. He suspects that the Mini was a delivery vehicle with a limited trade plate. Robert Black was a former delivery driver. In fact, he used his job to lure, rape, and kill his victims. Mr. Clark also said that the police should investigate Robert's driving history, since according to reports, he had been driving since 1964.

Missing People

Robert Black might be dead and he won't be indicted for April Fabb's disappearance, but if a lead is established then her family would have the closure and the Norfolk Constabulary would finally be able to solve their most puzzling case thus far.

Malcolm Cliver

Chapter 12 : Lost Keepers in Flannan Isles

Oceans are dangerous if you trudge it unprepared. It was believed that three lighthouse keepers from before were engulfed by the Atlantic Ocean. They were Thomas Marshall, Donald MacArthur and James Ducat.

Neglected Lighthouse

Thomas, Donald, and James were the assigned lighthouse keepers of the then newly opened lighthouse in Flannan Isles. Specifically, the islands were located in Outer Hebrides, Scotland. The building started in 1895 and was finished in 1899. At that time, the only communication was through light posts that were only visible from Hebrides during fine weather.

In 1925, though, they upgraded that communication system into wireless telegraphy. By that time however, the three lighthouse keepers were already missing for 25 years.

The unfortunate day was December 15, 1900. On that day, a wind storm struck the sea and many sailors sought guidance from the newly built lighthouse. However, they became mad when they realized that the Flannan Lighthouse was not being managed properly. They made

Missing People

this statement because, during the storm, no lights coming from the Flannan guided them. The sailors waited for any news on why the lighthouse was not operational, but because of the weather, the relief ship (Hesperus) was delayed.

When Joseph Moore, the keeper of the Hesperus saw the lighthouse from afar, he immediately felt that something was wrong. First of all, there was no one to greet them, which was a regulatory practice. The provision boxes to be restocked were also not prepared and the flag was not on the flagpole.

Unclear clues

When Moore and his other crew entered the lighthouse, nothing was amiss. The beds were undone, meaning they were slept on. The lamps were also cleaned because the ashes were evident. From Moore's observation, it was as if the guards or at least one of them, was in a hurry to leave.

This was because only one of the oilskins was left even though there were three sets of outdoor gear (for the three keepers). This meant that one of the guards left without a coat. That alone was suspicious: who would leave without outdoor gear when the weather was bad? On top of that, why would all of them leave at once?

All in all, the only protection the lighthouse had, was the

locked front door and gate. Moore became increasingly worried when none of the three lighthouse keepers attended to their arrival. As per the rule of the Northern Lighthouse Board, at least one of the keepers should manage the lighthouse-- that was why there were three of them. Leaving the post unattended was downright unethical. Because Moore believed that the keepers knew the rule by heart, he began to think that something must have happened to the three of them.

Without the keepers, Moore and some crew stayed in the Flannan Lighthouse to manage it, while Captain Harvie of the Hesperus led the ship back to the Breasclete. He also sent a letter to the Northern Lighthouse Board, telling them that something terrible happened to the Flannan Isles.

The Logbook

Staying in the lighthouse, Moore and his crew had more time to investigate what happened. They noticed that railway was scraped out of the concrete bedding and the iron railings were bent awkwardly. This got them thinking that the storm must have been stronger than they originally concluded. Their immediate theory was that all the keepers fell victim to the storm and they were engulfed by the ocean while trying to manage the lighthouse. However, when Moore found the logbook, he

Missing People

started having doubts.

On December 12, Thomas wrote that the storm was very strong. The waves were so high that they gashed at the lighthouse. He also said that in his lifetime, he had never seen such a raging storm. Later on the same day, he noted that the wind was becoming steady, and even though the storm was still strong, it was showing signs of subsiding. In the end, something was mentioned about how James Ducat was irritable and how he couldn't get out of the post due to the raging storm.

On December 13, the logbook read: the storm continued through the night. The wind shifted, James Ducat was quiet and MacArthur was praying. Later at noon, Thomas also said something about Grey Daylight, and how all of them were praying.

On December 14, there were no entries.

And finally, on December 15, logs were about how the storm was over and the sea turned calm. God was over them after all, according to Thomas. December 15 was the last entry of the logbook, and it was also on that evening when the sailors noticed that no guiding lights were coming from the Flannan Isles.

Due to this, investigations were carried out, but all their efforts were futile. No bodies were recovered and there was no sign of violence, except for the ones caused by the storm. They concluded that the logbook was a hoax-- first and foremost was the emotional writing. The log entries should have been objective: there shouldn't be writings that pertain to "praying" and being "irritable".

On top of that, it was suspicious how Thomas would input about Ducat's irritable attitude when Ducat was his superior. One log entry also said something about "MacArthur crying". For those who knew MacArthur, they would not believe it because the man was a brawler. Lastly, the entry about them praying was a total sham-- according to Superintendent Muirhead, who knew all three personally, none of the three keepers was a praying person.

If the log entries were truly hoaxes, then who wrote it and why would someone put in such effort?

Others argue that the emotional side of the entries could have been because of the stress they were experiencing due to the storm. Perhaps, that was why James Ducat was being irritable, and why they all prayed and realized that God was with them. Working in an isolated place could make their agreeable personalities clash.

Forever unsolved

No one will know what really happened to the three

Missing People

lighthouse keepers-- but one theory was accepted by many. It could be that two of the keepers were trying to manage the West landing, and when they experienced trouble, the one managing the lighthouse went to their rescue. This would explain why one oilskin was left behind. In the process, all three were washed away by the waves. We may never know.

Conclusion

Thank you again for purchasing this book!

Whatever happened to these people could be anyone's guess. Perhaps they were murdered, or maybe they sought freedom from what could be their unwanted life. Whatever the reason was for their disappearance, it will help a lot if their cases remain in the minds of the general population.

If you enjoyed this book, would you be kind enough to leave me a review on Amazon? Thank you so much, I truly do appreciate it!

Check Out My Other Books

Below you'll find some of my other popular books that are popular on Amazon and Kindle as well. You can visit my author page on Amazon to see other work done by me. (Malcolm Cliver).

Missing People

Hollywood Murders

If the links do not work, for whatever reason, you can simply search for these titles on the Amazon website, with my name to find them.

Malcolm Cliver

Want more books?

Would you love books delivered straight to your inbox every week?

Free?

How about non-fiction books on all kinds of subjects?

We send out e-books to our loyal subscribers every week to download and enjoy!

All you have to do is join! It's so easy!

Just visit the link below to sign up and then wait for your books to arrive!

www.LibraryBugs.com

Enjoy :)

Printed in Great Britain
by Amazon